Learning to Love Again

Jameel Muhammad

"Learning to Love Again"
By Jameel Muhammad

ISBN 978-0692708200

Copyright© 2016 HJM Publishing, LLC.
First published in the USA
By HJM Publishing, LLC. Atlanta, Ga
All rights reserved.

Cover designed by HJM Publishing LLC.
Formatting by Polgarus Studio

Website – www.jameelmuhammad.com
Follow me on Instagram – @jameel.muhammad.73
Follow me on twitter – @jameelmuhammad0
Follow me on Facebook –www.facebook.com/learning2loveagain

To my late, beloved mother, Velma Muhammad,
my first teacher and love.

Contents

Introduction

In the Name of God the Beneficent, the Merciful

Learning to Love Again

Thank you for attempting to open your mind and heart to a process and journey that will give you unspeakable joy and peace and happiness. It won't be easy, and you will have your ups and downs, but if you humbly walk this journey with me you will learn to love again in a way that absolutely frees your spirit to accept love and give love abundantly. This experience will come to you as naturally as breathing, for you will learn to tap into the source of infinite divine love, God himself.

This journey is a constant test of your will to be happy and loving again. Along this path you will tap into hidden creativity inside you and learn to channel emotions that will fuel your determination to heal. You will learn guiding principles to love in a manner that is fulfilling and that enables you to express love freely without fear.

Every chapter marks a major stage of growth for me in my eternal battle to perfectly reflect God's love. *Learning to Love Again* is a testament to my life of searching and discovering spiritual and emotional tools to heal from the pain and trauma of heartbreak and heartache. Every chapter was inspired by authentic experiences that spurred me to write and share with others what I was learning. In this journey I am your fellow traveler. So walk with me and allow my words to inspire, motivate, and lift you to heights that only true divine love can carry you to.

In the Name of God, the One Who Nourishes Us Through Our Pain with Divine Love, the Comforter, the Forbearer

The Beginning

How do you love again when your heart and dreams have been crushed under the weight of disappointment? We all enter this world trusting our benefactors, and our innocence knows no suffering from abandonment and betrayal. Whether we lose a loved one to death, separation, breakup or divorce, we have to find the strength to will ourselves to find peace and purpose through our tragedy.

Since I began writing to inspire my readers, they have become a facilitator of my own emotional salvation. Through this time I have experienced what I once felt was unfathomable, unconscionable: a divorce.

I never as a man thought I would go to the movies by myself, or worse, come out sobbing uncontrollably from a sappy movie like Will Smith's *Seven Pounds*. Love songs suddenly seemed to start talking to me and reflecting aspects of my plight, when before they were all just the melody of life. My religion as I knew it expanded from a socio-theological solution to become a personal conduit to happiness through the attainment of peace.

God was no longer limited to doing the work of the Good Samaritan that came to raise us (black people) from our wretched condition in America. He became the Savior I needed to find the reasons to smile and get through the day. As I experienced, God can allow everything you thought you loved to be taken away, stripping you to where you are a prayer and a phone call away from suffering depression.

But I thank God for His guidance to us through His servants, because they are real human beings who can offer comfort to you when you need it most. I reference God so much because having a clear concept of God is the only thing that I know I can rely on when I am extremely disappointed.

Today my religion represents learning to love again, trust again, and maintain happiness through my work of helping people. **Learning to love again started with redefining the reasons to love God and myself after my divorce.** I cannot overemphasize the importance of sincere prayer where you give up your ability to handle things and put it all on God's shoulders and release. In this supplication I specifically called on the God who is the Best Knower, whom I affectionately refer to as Protecting Best Friend, God in person.

When we are dejected it is best to focus on specific attributes of God that will manifest His power through us. It's imperative for us to express our epiphanies and spiritual insights through an artistic or creative medium. This exercise will help us heal faster by allowing us to feel less isolated and alone by relating constructively with others. It will also help others learn from your experience and feel encouraged to share their experiences with others. In applying this principle, I would sometimes study for hours or weeks and combine those efforts with my personal experiences to inspire my next writing. I was quietly starting to find the reasons to love again. Next I reached out to talk to people whom I felt shared my best interests. You will find the most comfort in talking to people who share your core values and common interests.

Although complaining and venting while being counselled might seem therapeutic to the wounded soul, it's far better to adopt a tone of solutions and personal commitment. Accepting responsibility is one of the Eight Steps of Atonement, and there can be no healing or love if we do not accept full responsibility for our thoughts and actions.

The Eight Steps of Atonement, carried out and practiced sincerely and with the guidance and help of God, are a giant leap in the right direction.

1. Someone must point out the wrong
2. Acknowledgement of wrong
3. Confess the fault; first to God, then to those offended
4. Repentance; a feeling of remorse or contrition or shame for the past conduct which was wrong and sinful
5. Atonement; meaning to make amends and reparations for the wrong
6. Forgiveness by the offended party; to cease to feel offense and resentment against another for the harm done
7. Reconciliation and restoration; meaning to become friendly and peaceable again
8. Perfect union with God and with each other

Asking "why" will yield different results every day depending on your mood, so I strongly suggest seeking God's guidance on your perception of events. When we are viewing our life emotionally we are looking at life from a selfish, vain perspective, but when we are submitting to God, who should be the center of our lives, we expand our breast to properly handle disappointment to forgive others and learn to love again.

Learning to love again means identifying with the part of you that is eternal and cannot be severely hurt and devastated again. This part is not emotional, it is the part of us that uses emotions to connect to that which does not lie or betray. When we are reconnecting to our God we are disconnecting ourselves from temporary happiness through instant gratification, titles, feelings or things and directing our focus toward the Author of Happiness, the Bestower of Permanent Peace, God. To love again we have to connect to God's essence — the original blueprint from which all of our souls originate. When we no longer feel like our purpose is to experience individual, temporary pleasure, but rather to share in a collective joy of happiness, cultivating and expressing the Creator's gifts to the service of humanity, we will truly learn to love again in a way where we will never experience the emotional severity of that pain again.

Jesus's first commandment says to love God with all your heart, mind, and soul. That means to free our heart's love from hurt and betrayal, it must be centered in God. Our emotions must be wrapped around the permanence of God's will. I personally never want to experience the depths of emotional anguish, confusion, and fury again. I am learning to love again with God as my center, while loving the people in my life as I focus on the best part in us that is in service to God's will.

In the Name of God, the Author of Love Who Created Us from His Image, the Originator of Friendship Who Embodies Love and the Active Will of the Creator in a Well-Made Man

Redefining Our Identity

As I write this, I am coming off a month of fasts and deep self-reflection, which was beautiful and inspiring. I admit I had good days and bad ones. Fasting has a way of bringing emotions out of you that you might not like. But it is wonderful to see yourself for who you are deep inside.

To learn to love again requires us to be broken down to our weakest point to see what or whom we turn to in order to validate ourselves. Who are we? What makes us happy? What is love? How we answer these questions determines how or if we ever learn to love again, because the responses define for us who we are as individuals.

When I was dealing with the intense pain of heartbreak I wanted to show myself that I still had *swag*. So at this point I immediately wanted to redefine who I was and how I appeared to the public. I thought by adopting a baller persona I would ultimately become happy again. WRONG! Instead, I discovered this rule for myself in the process: **We cannot find happiness and peace contingent on the approval or perception of others.**

Our identity is defined by our passion, conviction, and manifestation of that which we love and how we express it to others. Oftentimes we reshape our identity because we have experienced hurt or pain. One of the worst things we can do because of a bad breakup, or because we are hurt, is start doing things out of envy, jealousy, or betrayal. One of the best medicines known for a broken heart is to reacquaint yourself with what makes you happy. Your hobbies, your interests and talents remind you that you're still important and still valuable to yourself.

Showing gratitude through prayer for our gifts and talents will return us from the brink of depression and give us reasons to get out of bed. Our positive thoughts and actions have the power to recreate a new peaceful existence for us instantly. This process of revitalizing our well-being with positive and healthy thoughts helps us to learn to love again and reacquaint ourselves with the best part of our natures. We should replenish ourselves with a good mental and physical diet, which will assure us a healthy disposition.

Our anger can become our enemy! When we are furious over the circumstances of a breakup, it can cause us to become unbalanced. Unbridled frustration can make us dangerous to ourselves and others. We have to learn to channel our anger and negative emotions toward something that is constructive and non-detrimental to our growth and development. Although we might believe we are thinking rationally and dispassionately when we contemplate revenge toward an ex-loved one for hurting us, we are actually doing ourselves a disservice to harbor rage and consider retaliation because someone broke our heart.

There is a mistaken notion of entitlement that we have when we are enjoying the fruits of a relationship. As the saying goes, "tomorrow is not promised," so we can never assume that because we desire a relationship to prosper it must be destined to flourish despite all obstacles. We must be grateful for every moment and every day where we are able to enjoy the bliss of a loving relationship, and cherish the time we have with the person and people that are loving toward us.

Since God is the best knower, we can expect Him to understand how we feel and give us the best understanding when we turn to Him. Since God has risen above His emotions yet still has them, He can relate to us like no other being can. The process of handling a failed relationship can create anger, so it is vital for us to refer to Him for the answer. I can get through my moments of feeling deprived of fair treatment by a past loved one by reflecting on my faith in universal justice or *Ma-at*.

A human being ideally cannot love you more than he loves God and himself. Love for God has always been determined by our nearness to our duty to Him and ourselves. We have a duty to glorify God through our cultivation and resurrection of our human spirit. Our level of respect for the temple God gave to us to house His spirit also determines how much we love God. So we cannot expect a person who doesn't care much for their duty to their God or themselves to care so much about us. It is impossible.

This rule should help relieve us of some of the anger we have toward people who wrong us. When someone has settled on the worst part of their nature they are not operating out of divine love, they are functioning on an animalistic level where impulse and cravings begin to rule them.

I pray that all of us begin the journey to learn to love again righteously and peacefully. The road to being able to love again properly begins with the quiet peace of mind that is present in the darkness of night and stillness of the morning, not in entering a new relationship.

In the Name of God, the Most Trustworthy One on Whom We All Depend, the Source of Our Loving Divine Identity

Rebuilding Trust

Have you ever been hurt so badly you didn't know how or where you would find the strength to love and trust again? What was it about the experience that severely damaged you emotionally and traumatized you psychologically? Did losing someone disrupt your sense of security and happiness? Many of us struggle to trust people once we have been hurt. Since it seems trust is a very valuable commodity and trait, how is trust defined?

Trust:

1. Reliance on the integrity, strength, ability, surety, etc., of a person or thing; confidence
2. Confident expectation of something; hope

Almost all of us have been in relationships where our trust in someone was compromised severely and we then found ourselves teetering on the edge of completely doubting not only other people, but the very idea and concept of someone being trustworthy.

Before you become another sad victim of somberness, bitterness, and doubt, please allow the insights I have discovered to help you regain, reclaim, and rebuild the desire to love and trust another human being.

The only way to seek refuge from the kind of pain that comes from betrayal is to confide in the God of Trust, the Source of Trust, and the only one that we can wholeheartedly put all of our hope, faith, and trust in — the Trustee of Our Hearts — God Himself.

That is where all healing begins and ends. When we have placed our will, our deepest hopes, dreams, and aspirations squarely on the shoulders of God Himself, the only being worthy of such absolute dependence, then we free ourselves of worry, doubt, and undue suspicion. No relationship is worthy of the absolute devotion that should be given to God; however, to learn to trust again we must embrace the opportunity to challenge our fear of being disappointed by others.

As I transformed my post-divorce identity, I was forced as a man to attach to no idea, dream, or aspiration of love and security that is outside of fulfilling my divine purpose. The idea of a loving family or career must be completely subsumed by our service and submission to the author of our divine identity.

We must reformulate our identities and what constitutes our self-worth to stand on the only foundation that will never crack or falter under the weight of expectation and disappointment. We can no longer define ourselves by the circumstances of our past.

To love and trust again, our identities must be broken down and reoriented from all of the images of television, magazines, and talk shows that have infected our minds with the idea of personal happiness and success devoid of true divine inspiration and guidance. We cannot predict the precise moment when God will bless us to attract someone we earnestly desire. Real love — not the transitory sensation of infatuation — comes from God based on His plan for us. Despite what we have been led to believe, there is no replacement for patience.

Patience:

1. The quality of being patient, as the bearing of provocation, annoyance, misfortune, or pain, without complaint, loss of temper, irritation, or the like
2. An ability or willingness to suppress restlessness or annoyance when confronted with delay: to have patience with a slow learner
3. Quiet, steady perseverance; even-tempered care; diligence: to work with patience

But fear not. Patience never means idly waiting. Patience involves the quiet work of desiring, attracting, and becoming that which our hearts truly yearn for. So if we want real love we are going to have to become a real loving person ourselves. When God produces the right atmosphere of inner peace and tranquillity in our lives, we are bound to attract the kind of people who resonate and vibrate on our same spiritual wavelength.

Our identities must be reshaped and revamped to fit new ideas of love that are not rooted in false images of masculinity and femininity.

These ideas must be instilled educationally, morally, and spiritually from a clear self-concept free from baggage of subliminal pain that haunts us like ghosts from our past.

When our identities line up with the Supreme Being we put ourselves on a course of perfection that draws us out of emotionalism — and to the thinking and mind of God.

Emotionalism:

1. A tendency to display or respond with undue emotion, esp. morbid emotion.
2. Unwarranted expression or display of emotion.

I want you all to find love, happiness, and trust in your lives. I know that we all have to have a clear definition of what we want and clear steps to get there to have a measure of peace in our lives.

In the Name of God, the Life-Giver and Restorer of Love, Peace and Happiness in Wounded Souls

Taking Emotional Inventory

How are you doing in your soul's quest to heal, and learn to love again? It is imperative to track your overall progress in learning to love again by measuring your ability to trust again and be truly at peace with yourself and God. Have you ever noticed that you can have all the right sayings in your head and be a good adherent of your faith and still find yourself unable to liberate yourself completely of inner turmoil, stress, and sin? Unfortunately, this is the case for most of us.

I've found many of us have deep-seated emotions that we put in the back of our minds and refuse to deal with properly. When you have loved someone and they have hurt you and disappointed you it is healthy to give yourself proper time to heal, meditate, and contemplate what will bring complete peace in your life. Getting a calendar and marking it off by the days you have successfully completed by employing productive habits to channel your feelings will give you a tangible measure to show you your progress.

Although we may watch the calendar roll by if we are not taking the proper steps to relieve ourselves of the stress, anger, bitterness, guilt and negative emotions associated with our past, we are not doing ourselves justice, and we are deluding ourselves into believing we are prepared to love again if we are not.

Well, how do you know if you are suffering from something? You check for symptoms. We should ask ourselves the following questions and attempt to answer them as truthfully as possible:

Do we find ourselves thinking about our past relationships in awkward moments? Do we find ourselves sadly glued to the couch when we have things to do? Are we constantly engaging in meaningless relationships to keep from being lonely? Do we commit self-destructive acts to get away from painful thoughts? Do we associate with negative people to reinforce our negative stereotypes of our past loved ones?

If you suffer from any of those symptoms, don't feel bad—it does not mean you are a bad or weak person. We can have the best of hearts and still suffer from the emotional anguish related to these unresolved questions and situations. The key is to identify the relationship problems you have experienced and start to work on resolving them using the steps of this book to learn to love again.

Your negative experiences are not there to haunt you and torment you forever. They are there for you to go through to appreciate and learn the value of God in your life.

The secret to dealing with pain is to not run from it but run toward it. Some thoughts become objects that depress your spirit when you deny, suppress or feel ashamed of them. Hatred is the opposite of love and is dependent on an intense emotional attachment to fuel its drive in you.

Most hatred or anger you have toward a past loved one is a sign that you still love them, whether you like it or not. Oh no, don't beat me up! But it is true, and it is also natural. When circumstances lead to two people separating it does not mean they won't still have love for each other, no matter what led to the separation. Didn't we love being younger? We don't have to negate the positivity of our past to accept the fact we're older and more mature now.

It is the same with whoever played a part in shaping us and helping us grow to where we are today. If we accept our feelings and release the negative energy attached to them we can embrace the reality of the present and future of our lives.

The hardest thing to do is to admit to yourself that someone hurt you and then you forgive them for it. The best thing to do to be able to move on with your life is forgive people who hurt you more than you would like to admit.

Learning to love again is a process that takes being honest with ourselves, God, and everyone else. Our success actually depends on our properly handling our negative emotions. Take your negative emotions and release them. One of the best ways to channel your negative emotions positively is to help someone else who is going through what you went through so you both can be happy and not bitter. Don't you want to love without limits and conditions again and feel free? Practice atonement and spread the spirit to someone else. Together we will learn to love again with each other's help.

In the Name of God, the Forbearer, the Life Giver, the One Who Created Himself and Embodies His Spirit in Flesh as a Mercy to Those of Us Who Are of the Flesh

Reestablishing the Foundation to Love Again

If you have been fighting on the battlefield of relationships, you probably have become a casualty of love and have had to bear the wound of a broken heart and disappointment sometime in your life. I have. A friend told me that as a man you know you've been brokenhearted if you've ever cried your eyes out in the fetal position. Whoa, that's pain! I am sure women can relate to that kind of indescribable and heart-wrenching pain, too.

When my heart was shattered to pieces, I began to fall into an abyss of self-loathing before I found solace in the only one I can trust, and that is God Himself. He understands our pain because of His direct relationship to us. During my agony I cried out to God to comfort me, and my prayers were answered because of my faith.

The lesson is there is an opportunity to love again in a way that ultimately brings us closer to God and brings us peace and trust. To the heartbroken, the subject of trust conjures up feelings of grief and disappointment. When we are learning to love again we are learning how to trust ourselves and each other again. But how do we do that? We have to turn to God in prayer and complete submission to ask Him to release us from the bondage and crippling effect of the pain or guilt we suffer. We are asking God to take us and show us a way through His mercy to be grateful to the one whom we can trust, depend and rely on completely, God Himself. When we turn to Him we are able to appreciate the blessings in our life despite our pain and reconnect to the source of life, happiness and love.

We mark a phase of our spiritual growth in this process when we are learning to view people through the lens of their divine traits rather than through their faults and shortcomings. In spite of being victimized by individuals in our past, we must establish the emotional fortitude to be determined to settle on the best part of people. The best part in people is a reflection of their divine gifts and attributes. It is easier to recognize the goodness in other people when we see it within ourselves and express it through our character. It's possible to forgive others who have hurt us and love once more when we rearrange our thinking to place God in the center of our hearts like the sun and let the radiance of our love of Him shine on other people.

We have been stepped on by bad relationships. But the purpose is to show us something in ourselves that is human and divine and needs its Creator to guide it and shape it to its spiritual maturity. I never thought I would have to learn to love again, but personal development demanded that I improve the manner in which I approach all my relationships. Our emotional and spiritual immaturity must be overcome to reach a point where we don't let our negative personal circumstances compromise our good nature and sense of well-being and make us emotionally unstable.

We all want to experience life with as much ease as possible, but our soul unconsciously seeks to reconnect to our essence in God Himself. When we look up from the circumstance of our lives we see a world, a universe in motion that will move without us if we don't get in synch with the Creator's will for our lives. We must re-evaluate our selfish motives to desire love and companionship. God wants us to wrap our emotions and our natural desire to be happy and in love around pleasing Him first through our spiritual, moral, and civic obligations to one another. When the establishment and perpetuation of truth and good values is at the center of our desire for personal fulfilment, then our love is not suffocating from selfish motives. So how do you clear your conscious of the negative emotions associated with your current or former loved ones?

You have to learn the lessons from your relationship that will prepare you to be a more loving, caring person.

Can or will we ever learn to trust again when someone has badly hurt us? Only the individual can answer that question, because it is a question of the heart and desire. But we can definitely start the process of regaining our ability to trust people coming into our lives again if we allow ourselves to recognize and appreciate their virtues. We can develop the ability to trust other people by supporting positive action from people who help our families and communities. We should trust the outcome of the good works and deeds done by people even if we are unsure about their intentions for committing them because God is the ultimate judge of people's hearts. In *Learning to Love Again,* we are learning to build trust by strengthening our bond and trust in God Himself first and foremost to be the spiritual steward of our lives and relationships. From there we place our faith and love in Him and allow ourselves to reflect His love and compassion in others by becoming more virtuous and following His guidance.

In the Name of God, the most Majestic, the Noblest, the Exalted One.

Accepting Our Divinity

Just like most of my readers, I have been greatly unjust to myself in running from my own divinity and purpose. Through my growth and mistakes I have learned spiritual solutions that we might all use to learn to love the right way, and not the way that constantly leads to pain, sorrow, and heartbreak.

What makes us lie, betray, and become dishonest with the ones we love? Is it because we are scared to trust that God will reward our faith? Why do we blame others for our failures to pursue our passions and dreams? Why do we hold our occupational titles or social positions as indicators of our righteous, moral, and civic value? Should we wait for that job, car, house, girlfriend, boyfriend, or spouse as an authorization to be true to ourselves and our families?

No. Our material possessions or labels do not define our spiritual identities. Our true identities cannot be defined by the temporary conditions in our lives, because we are constantly growing and changing. The heart must accept its relationship to the Creator to have any measure of faith in its destiny to discover its divine purpose, a path which leads to all that we truly need and desire to be happy. Without an inkling of understanding of the full reality of God, we must still have faith in what we struggle to comprehend of His infinite love and compassion for us. Accepting Him as our Protecting Friend who can hug us and love us when no one else can is truly exercising faith in Him. The awareness of our divinity is our connection to His Presence. When we are being sneaky and conniving it is His love for us that allows us to be exposed, not to degrade us, but to uplift us with the assurance that it is God who manifests all truth.

Learning to Love Again is not just about suffering as a victim of circumstance. It is about accepting responsibility for our duty to God and our loved ones, and realizing how we have fallen short and must do better to have peace. Accepting our righteous nature is absolutely necessary to embark on the journey to reclaim our divinity and self-assurance, which is the only path to lasting peace, because neither money nor fame has ever completely satisfied one's soul. Accepting our divinity means taking our crown of righteous nobility and wearing it with the honor of a king or queen and the humility of a servant. God could destroy us for our misdeeds through the acts of others or Nature if He were not merciful and compassionate to us. When we can accept the divinity in ourselves we can start to recognize it, appreciate it, and treat other people like we should view ourselves.

We must stop looking for people to occupy our time, but rather turn to God in solitude if we are to reestablish that bond that is greater than any pain that can be inflicted. We must stay away from the herd of negative people who, out of their apathy toward moral uprightness and family, will manipulate us into being dishonest with ourselves and loved ones. Those who have denied their own divinity will always drag us to the same immorality and depravity if we let them. Our divinity is the gift we have to connect to the Creator's Will. To ignore it, or worse, to deny it by our actions, is to sentence our lives to an empty existence of vanity that will forever be dependent on others' approval of what we have.

We are to love God with all our heart and soul and ask Him to guide our heart back to where it belongs. Ask Him to forgive us for our shortcomings and make us be better. Stay away from philosophies that absolve one of personal responsibility and a God-centered approach to relationships. Men don't completely know women, and women don't completely know men, so it is unproductive to engage in discussions that do not acknowledge the dynamic nature of male-female relationships. We must study ourselves and fall in love with our higher selves or Divinity to approach love with maturity. Our natures complement one another because of our differences and similarities. Our souls and nature demand a polarity in the opposite sex that will MAKE us become better people. Although there are many relationship alternatives that can satisfy an urge for intimate companionship, this prescription to recognize and embrace our divinity helps men and women, who not only need each other to procreate but also to spiritually mature and connect to the One God who created us in pairs in the beginning. To run from that reality is to run from the purpose for which we were created. An unbalanced appetite for sexual gratification will ruin us and reduce us to the level of a beast — or even lower — where we will be blinded to the divinity within the opposite sex. Our divinity is a guide to help us behold His attributes, which unfold through the experience of loving one another.

In the Name of God, Who Comforts the Soul and Gives It Everlasting Peace

Words to Live By

In an offering of spiritual food to feed the wounded soul striving to be upright in a wicked world, I present these expressions to be taken to heart:

Letting Go and Let God — Isolating ourselves in our weakest moments and earnestly calling on the God we believe in to deliver us from our painful circumstances.

Releasing ourselves from the bondage of sin entails coming face-to face with our worst nightmares.

There was a time when The Originator desired another being like Himself. Loneliness is now required for all of us to conquer to know Him who Created Himself with no Consort or Companion.

Guilt will destroy you if do not know how to forgive yourself when no one else will. Atone SINCERELY to God first, yourself second, and your loved ones third. If your loved ones do not forgive you don't try to make them, you have done all you can. Be patient and leave it in the hands of God.

Drugs, alcohol, sex or any combination thereof have never effectively soothed a broken heart. You will be tortured with guilt afterward and wish you had just faced your problems clear-minded, sober, and celibate.

Striving to be righteous is not perfection, it is the humble practice of removing all obstacles that stand in your way to become one with God.

Men, it is better to cry than to lie to yourself and others that you are not in pain. Release your tears, because God counts every drop shed by the Righteous.

Even a hypocrite's good deeds will be rewarded, so don't waste time judging the hearts of others, especially when you have not exceeded them in good works.

Only a living God with a loving heart can hear your prayer and have the power, compassion, and mercy to come to your aid when you need Him the most.

The greatest love is unconditional like a mother loving her child. Real love is eternal regardless of time, place, or circumstance.

Anger is cancer that destroys its carrier from the inside.

Anger is an emotion that requires complete adherence. If we are unbalanced, harboring anger can destroy our lives and the lives of others.

Anger must be channeled to positive aggressive behavior. Exercise is one of the best methods to channel it. Doing a creative task is another.

Acceptance of a situation requires acknowledgement of the actual facts. Avoid appeasing your ego or you will succumb to anger easily.

Hate is the opposite of love. It takes an incredible amount of negative energy to hate anything because it requires a destructive nature to channel it.

There is a time to defend yourself and go to war with the emotional pain within. Identify the enemy within yourself that is keeping you from being happy and at peace. God loves those who struggle and fight against their own weaknesses and shortcomings.

You don't have time to debate who is God when facing your death.

Decide who He is to you so He can be an empowering force before it is too late.

A sincere prayer will calm the grieving heart. Read your choice of scripture to talk to Him.

Run toward the pain in your life to face it head-on. Be committed to overcoming it with God's help only, and no substitute.

Morality is the ladder to spirituality. Fleshly desires must be mastered and overcome to transcend them.

Loving a moral law is to derive personal satisfaction from practicing it and detaching it from vanity.

Moral laws give us the freedom to be righteous when we have been in bondage to our sin and weakness.

Everyone is capable of some type of creativity because it is the signature gift of God in us.

There is nothing more powerful than a determined will possessed by a disciplined righteous person.

I hope these words have inspired you to be a stronger, upright person. They were composed as I turned within myself to meet and overcome the obstacles in my life. They are the thoughts that have comforted me in my time of distress and disappointment. Let these thoughts impress upon you an unparalleled commitment to self-improvement and positive change.

In the Name of God, the Embodiment of Love in a Well-Made Man

Letting Go

Once we begin the journey to learn to love again, we reach a point where we are getting closer to expunging our hearts of the bitterness and disappointment that poison our spirit and depress our soul. At this junction is the crossroads where we can plunge into despair and grief or swim into the bliss of happiness, forgiveness, and love. These contrasting possibilities — the negativity, doubt, and pain of the past versus the hope, excitement, and promise of peace of our future — occupy our minds as warring enemies, incompatible and viciously opposed to one another.

This crossroads is our present where the summation of our experiences, beliefs, hopes and dreams will influence our consciousness to choose our life's direction. So where are we going, and how are we going to get there if we continue to hold emotional baggage of unresolved or unaccepted issues? Simply, we are going to LET GO and hold on to the one thing, idea, principle, purpose, and person that is eternal, God Himself. Our family, our loved ones, our best friends will disappoint us, hurt us, or even betray us to where we become cold and bitter and lose faith that God upholds a moral justice that rewards honor, loyalty and trust in righteousness.

How do we let go when we want to atone? How do we let go when we want forgiveness or want the other person to atone and make amends with us? We Let Go! Sometimes that means putting aside our pride and reputation and humbling ourselves to God and our loved ones. Sometimes that means turning away from the substitutes of happiness — drugs, alcohol, casual sex, etc. Sometimes that means picking yourself up from the stupor of self-pity and depression, and getting active doing the things you love that are righteous. Letting go sometimes means being patient and allowing God to send you someone instead of degrading yourself at bars and clubs for attention and companionship. Most important, letting go requires us to challenge our fear of loneliness and rejection and turn ourselves completely to the Originator of the heavens and earth.

Letting go requires us to stand on the rock of our morality, faith, and purpose. We can't let go if we feel like we have no one or nothing to turn to. We all need to feel secure emotionally and physically. The trial, the temptation of our lower selves to rationalize immorality, and even hypocrisy, occurs when we are faced with the apparent lack of genuine companionship. We begin to gravitate toward whomever shows us good or bad attention, because of our sense of insecurity when left alone with our feelings of rejection and humiliation.

We need not fret or worry any longer as we stand on the rock of our faith in God's power to free us from pain, a position from where we can let go and heal our hearts from our past transgressions. In this state we are learning to love the way God intended, where the love is free from the seeds of doubt, suspicion, and impatience. Learning to love again is allowing God to make you feel innocent and deserving enough of another opportunity to be happy with someone, no matter your past or current circumstances.

One of the toughest challenges we have in this process is our desire for someone else to pick up where the other person left off, denying ourselves the opportunity to have a clean slate and a fresh start. I know letting go is not easy, and for many it takes a lifetime, if ever, but we have an opportunity to do it right now. But you can't do it without God's help. Many people have tried unsuccessfully to replace their loved ones without turning to the Creator to heal. The first thing to do is realize that it is a process that starts with a commitment to self-discipline and steadfastness.

Accept your feelings. Know when you are under siege and subject to an emotional breakdown and call out to God to deliver you at that moment. Exercise, pray regularly, and turn your life into a charitable expression of your gratitude to God. Set yourself on a ninety-day course of action where you keep a journal and track your progress through your emotional report card. The success of our lives is contingent on our achieving permanent happiness and peace. If we let go and learn to love again with God backing us, He will protect our hearts and allow us to find peace, love, and tranquility inside and with others once again.

In the Name of God the Beneficent, the Most Merciful Savior

Self-Validation

If we are learning to let go of our past we must still find a way to uncover a self-identity that will accept the person who was hurt or disappointed by the last experience. This validation does not require any outside influence to confirm, sanction, or approve of the new person we are striving to be. The emotionally matured identity develops outside of the natural comfort of previous companionships, because the prior relationships could reinforce negative self-images that inhibit us from learning to love properly.

Learning to love again starts with rediscovering how to love ourselves when we are constantly growing and changing. What once gave us joy may fade over time, so we have to take time to discover what we like to do that reflects our growth and experience. Accepting and loving ourselves is the hardest, yet most fulfilling journey we could ever undertake. The reason the process is so challenging is because the moment we think we know ourselves, we change, and the process of self-validation and rediscovery continues. One mistake we make in the growth process is we often resort to immature behavior to enter new relationships. Some of us go back to the club or bar to hang out. We try to date and pick up exactly where we left off, not taking into account we are different now.

Learning to love again takes into account you are a transitional spiritual being, and how you think, talk, dress, and behave must reflect your evolving spiritual/emotional state or you won't have any peace of mind. Have you ever noticed that drinking with friends can become an addiction? It is not that the alcohol is so powerful, but naturally over time we assign emotional and physical substitutes as habits to compensate for the pain and disappointment we have had and continue to experience.

In our journey to validate ourselves we resort to things that in our past might have brought us great times and joy. However, as we mature our desire for casual intimacy wanes if we have become accustomed to monogamous relationships. Self-validation begins with identifying who we are becoming and who we were in the past and designing a lifestyle that will give us a lasting peace of mind. I believe that most of us are at a point where we know what we want, but we are too impatient to allow God to bring it to us without resorting to some vices.

So what if God doesn't bless us to find the one we are looking for in the next year or two or within the immediate future? Does that mean that we will settle for an amoral existence where we subsist off temporary lovers and vices to bide the time? In the formation of our identity, we have to decide who we are going to be regardless of anyone else in or out of our lives. Self-validation is about standing on principles and not allowing circumstances to makes us **emotionally dishonest** with ourselves.

Are we happy with ourselves? Sure, we can all claim heaven is at our feet, but we all know what we are doing individually that is breaking our peace. We have been hurt and we've hurt other people. We have been lied to and cheated on. We have been the one lying and cheating. Accepting ourselves is learning to love that person in the mirror who has been your best friend and worst enemy at the same time. When we can accept the worst part of ourselves but have chosen to settle on the best part of us that strives to be moral and righteous, then we can learn to accept it in others. Patience and love are qualities that are best measured within, because we can only have love and patience with each other if we love and have patience with our own faults and shortcomings.

Self-validation involves accepting the fact that you have emotionally hurt others and need to atone for it, then accepting the fact that people have emotionally damaged you and forgiving them.

Learning to love again is being aware of your faults and other people's faults and loving those people despite their shortcomings. It is rediscovering the new person who is maturing into a reflection of the Most High and molding a lifestyle that reflects that new individual. It is acceptance, forgiveness, and most of all love. We are all on this journey together, so learn to be more loving and patient with one another as we transition in our spiritual journeys.

In the Name of God, the Evolver Who Nourishes His Creation Stage after Stage until It Reaches Its Eventual Perfection

How to Love Ourselves

We all say that we love ourselves, right? Of course! But our self-love is intertwined with the outcome of relationships we have been part of. The journey of being in love can bruise us, batter our self-esteem and self-worth, and force us to ask the soul-wrenching questions, "Why me?" and "Why did I have to go through what I went through?" There is no generic answer or cliché that could possibly speak to the unique experience that each individual must endure to find himself.

We would have to stop talking and complaining about our circumstances to be able to answer the pivotal why-me question without coming to a vain, self-absorbed conclusion. When the question is asked to find resolution, peace, and to prepare you for the future, it is possible to approach the answer. When we approach our relationship trials with the proper perspective, we are able to understand their cause by deeply reflecting on our past.

Memories like the first time we fell in love must be enjoyed and let go with the promise of the present and faith in tomorrow's gift of the unknown. First, we have to believe in the possibility of love and become a daily witness of its power to rejuvenate and transform our lives. Second, we must release our feelings of guilt and betrayal or become prisoners of rage, sorrow, and vindictiveness, which sabotage any of our opportunities for happiness. Finally, we must become practitioners of real love, which is divine in nature from the source from which it springs.

In this phase of learning to love again we are taken into the depth of our spiritual journey, where we experience moments of happiness and wallow in grief in faster intervals than ever before. We have to open the door to accepting our divinity, find peace with our past, and seek validation from the only reality, God himself. Seeking relief with emotional substitutes and instant gratifiers such as drugs, alcohol, and casual sex unfortunately only sedates our mind into believing that we are happy, when we are actually neglecting our spiritual obligations to ourselves.

Learning to love ourselves again is now predicated on our knowledge and experience of witnessing ourselves in our most euphoric moments and our weakest points. When we discover the limits of what we are capable of doing under any amount of influence or distress, we are able to translate our self-awareness into self-love. As we go through trials our character reveals itself to us, and our God becomes intrinsic and vital to us as our Best Guide and Companion to overcome the tremendous emotional burdens we face. The more we strive to love again properly, the closer we are drawn to the source of all love, God Himself, who attracts others who are also revolving in the circle of light, life, and power. Our peace comes from that self-awareness, and our love for other human beings becomes infinite individual expressions reflecting our universal divine love for God Himself.

Learning to love again involves loving from a higher perspective that removes the vanity of selfishness. It is as valuable and in infinite abundance as the air we breathe; it cannot be hoarded, saved, or excluded for any particular group or time. It is based on the universal righteous principles of God Himself and can be shared, enjoyed, and encountered by any who chose to act upon it. Learning to love ourselves makes us become a better asset to our Creator, family, friends, community, and loved ones. It turns our "Why me?" into "Why not me?" Our experiences then become fertilizer to replant the seeds of love in our heart so our divine purpose may be realized.

When our prayers and devotional praise take on a greater meaning than performing religious rites, and our habits and behavior become much more than mundane expressions of our existence, then we are finding purpose for every second of our lives to show our love to Him and ourselves. Learning to love again becomes a prerequisite for spiritual growth and happiness when the heart is freed from past negative experiences. To neglect this spiritual reality is to allow ourselves to succumb to bitterness and perpetual grief.

We start loving ourselves by communicating positive thoughts to ourselves and others. Ask God to show you how to love yourself and free your heart of the rancor of pain and disappointment. Next show yourself and God that you are grateful for the vessel He has blessed you with and start taking care of it to express your newfound self-love. Feed your mind and body with the right spiritual and physical food that will affirm that you love God and yourself as one. Learning to love ourselves is the most vital process in our journey to love again. Our openness to clear ourselves to love again reflects our readiness to attract a mate into our lives.

Our dominant thoughts attract things to us. So we will attract inevitably the circumstances that reflect the thoughts we have harbored. So even if we don't know how to love ourselves truly, we can try, and we will gradually find more and more things we can do to enhance our mood, and love life. One of the greatest fulfilments is when two people can love each other while completely being themselves. So let's work on accepting our natural self and being ourselves so others can love the intelligent, healthy, ambitious, compassionate, successful people we are.

In the Name of God, the Embodiment of Love in a Living Being, the Noblest One, the Healer of Wounded Souls, the Mender of Broken Hearts

Accepting Happiness

I am forever grateful to God to have experienced this journey of love, because through the pain and turmoil I have learned to be happier than ever before. I marked the first anniversary of my divorce by beginning to write about love and healing. It was a starting point to access the damage that had been done to me and show I was determined to find a reason to smile inside again. Every one of us has to regain and discover the root of happiness within ourselves and find an outlet to express our unique creativity that will release our emotions in a positive, productive manner. We have to paint the reasons God loves us on the canvas of our countenance, transforming our innocent smiles into divine affirmations of purpose.

Before we can learn to love anyone else or ourselves properly we have to learn why God loves us in the first place. What made us so special that God would pattern our seemingly mundane genesis after His own self-creation in the womb of triple darkness? Why would He imbue each of our souls with a unique combination and ratio of his attributes? Discovering who we are in relation to God Himself requires us to thoroughly examine our physical, mental, and spiritual attributes in the light of our Creator's purpose for giving us life.

Have you asked yourself lately what you like to do and why you like to do it? What kind of impact do you want to have on your friends, family, classmates, colleagues, and peers? Can you write down ten reasons why God loves you right now? Discovering the reasons why we can and should love again starts with breaking through the fear and self-doubt that imprisons our emotions and keeps us from expressing happiness. If I may, I will define love with a citation from the Honorable Elijah Muhammad's teachings: "Love is the freedom to be justified expressing our purpose as to become equal with everything in God's creation." Learning to love again removes the selfish, egotistical view of love that is conditional on the satisfaction of our needs, thereby evolving into a divine outlook and expression of God's spirit that attracts and extracts the best part in human beings whenever it contacts them. Well, what is the best part of people? In a woman it is her feminine nature that passionately and freely surrenders her will to do the will of God to become His reflection of righteousness, beauty, wisdom, and mercy in an exquisite form irresistible to man's nature. In men it is their masculine nature that submits humbly to God's will to manifest and become a conduit of His wisdom, beneficence, power and sovereignty as His vicegerent.

The best parts in us are our gifts and interests that express our divine purpose. When we are learning to love again we acknowledge the poor part of ourselves, but we are choosing to settle on the best parts of ourselves and others that bring us closer to God in character and speech. Accepting our happiness is accepting that part of us that brings us joy and excitement in life. When we do what we love we attract people who will inevitably love us for being ourselves.

Well, how do we know we can ever find true happiness and love in someone else again? In a simple but powerful word: faith. But faith must be strengthened with prayer, fasting, and positive thinking. People who believe and say that there are no good men and women out there are right because they will never attract that which they don't believe exists.

The possibility of love must germinate like a seed in your heart to blossom into the fruit of your desires. Our faith in the source and bestower of love carries us, through patience and with perseverance. With God's help, it will be the constant conscious thought of doing His will and purpose that strengthens our faith that He will bless us with a helpmeet to aid us in His divine plan. The possibility of love manifests once there has been closure and rebirth in our lives. A sign that we are approaching an emotional rebirth is when our new encounters with people are now marked by our unconditional attempt to learn about and accept people for who they are with no expectations and requirements for their future roles in our lives.

Dating is discouraged in this process, because it hampers genuine communication without expectations.

I pray that my words have instilled desire to learn more on how to love again. I promise you that if you try to learn to love again properly, your fear of disappointment and heartbreak will disappear and you will tap into the infinite abundance of divine love that is in each and every one of us, which is more potent, and powerful than conditional love ever was.

This chapter is inspired by a period in my life that has witnessed pain, self-examination, and growth. With the help of God, my friends and readers, I feel free now to tap into a new well of abundance, joy, and happiness that has sprung forth through my journey to learn to love again. I am thankful for every kind word, warm greeting, and unexpected phone call I received from my friends that cheered me up to continue on this quest. Hopefully, through my words I can help others learn to love in a manner that transforms the student into a living expression of divine love, peace, and happiness.

In the Name of God, the Gentle One, Who Desires Happiness to Enter Our Hearts and Minds

Happiness Realized

What does it mean to accept happiness in our lives? It is to recognize and appreciate the things and people that give us joy every day. Innumerable factors can cause us to focus on the negative things that have happened to us in our relationships. Losing a loved one due to divorce, death, or any circumstance can create a void in our lives that keeps us harboring negative emotions. The easiest way to start living a fulfilling life and learning to love again is to identify the things that make you happy so your mind can be free to explore happiness through the activities that continually bring you joy and peace in your life.

You are stronger than you think you are. You have survived heartbreak and hopefully willed your way to a point of resolve where you are optimistic about the future. Regardless of what you have been through, if you have lived to talk about it you have an opportunity to not only overcome whatever painful relationship you have been in, but preserve and flourish in new fulfilling relationships with a new outlook and excitement. Even if fate has dealt you the most horrific circumstances you can will yourself to be whole again, loving, caring and giving.

You are finding contentment in your own solitude. There is no relationship with someone else than can replace being happy with yourself. Learning to love again first starts with learning to properly love yourself and then others. You cannot love yourself if you don't appreciate having time to nestle in your own thoughts and find a measure of peace. Simply looking in the mirror and being happy with the person you are looking at and becoming is worth smiling for. You cannot find joy in yourself if you are not actively seeking to learn and cultivate your interests, skills, and gifts God has placed in you for the benefit of yourself and humanity. There is only one of you, and the more you value that fact, the more of an asset you will be to yourself and others in a relationship.

You have fulfilling work and hobbies to do. The work you like to do brings you joy and happiness when you do it even if it is frustrating at times. It is so important to realize that the key to actualizing happiness in your life is to be actively doing the things and activities that you honestly enjoy. The secret in discovering like-minded people who can potentially become friends or loved ones is to immerse yourself in exactly what you love to do with your time. The wonderful truth is that whatever endeavor you like, there is probably someone else who enjoys it too. People who love what they do and do what they love are a joy to be around. They're fun and approachable, and they keep their life humming with new exciting opportunities and challenges to share.

You once dreamed of being where you are today. You're hopefully taller, stronger, and more independent, and you can do things that you once imagined. It doesn't matter what it is, or how insignificant it may seem, it is a goal realized and worth smiling about. Why? Many people have never had an opportunity to do many things you do and take for granted. If you have your motor skills, five senses, and can take care of yourself you are what millions of people throughout the world wish they had. So it is time to take inventory of your life and count your blessings, because most important, you have all the faculties and resources to solve your own problems of accepting happiness and learning to love in a way that is more fulfilling.

You have healthy relationships in your life. Learning to love again is predicated on learning to appreciate and be more loving in all of your relationships, whether they are romantic or not. To accept happiness in your life, you have to start building on good, functional relationships that bring joy in your life. Whether it is a family member or an old friend from childhood, there is somebody in your life who values you and appreciates your company. Take time to let them know that you appreciate them and recognize their intrinsic value to your life. Learning to love again is not just about learning to love those whom you have a romantic interest in; it is learning to share and express kindness to people who genuinely care about you. It is becoming a better friend, coworker, family member. It is the revitalization of your spirit to become a more loving person overall.

You have guidance to share. You have been through enough in life to help someone not make the same mistakes you have made. Whatever fate has brought you, it is for you to learn the lessons and share them with others. You are on the road to overcoming the hardships in your life by extracting the lessons to be learned, applying them to improve your life and sharing them with others.

You are content with your life right now and optimistic about the future. In order to accept happiness in your life there has to be a healthy balance of both outlooks. You can't be so hard on your life today that you by default plan to be miserable tomorrow. Whatever moments you have shared that brought joy in your life in your past, you should treasure them. They are your memories and no one can take them from you. However, you should take advantage of the present to create more pleasant memories, because the future is never promised for anyone, and there is no time like the HERE and NOW to start making a difference in your life and the lives of others.

You notice and appreciate little things in your life. You smile when you see the jubilant expression on a baby's face. You feel invigorated after a morning jog or workout. It is truly the little things in life that make it worth living. You take time to notice the quintessential beauty of the sunrise and the celestial sky at night. Once you realize that the best things in life are timeless, abundant, and free, you start to accept happiness in your life like never before.

Your passion in life makes you interesting to yourself and others. Your strong conviction for whatever you believe in attracts others to you and gives you a sense of purpose of being. If you show passion for what really concerns you and interests you, it uplifts you and helps you heal from bad relationships. When you are passionate about things that interest you, it's easy to find someone else who shares your passion or has similar interests as you. Surround yourself with people who are passionate about things you care about, and you will hardly ever have a dull moment in life.

You sense a purpose for being beyond your own existence. There is nothing more gratifying than to positively affect the lives of others. It nurtures your soul and gives you real happiness to know that your contribution to people's lives is a small thread in the cosmic fiber of humanity. Your altruism motivates and inspires you to have an invulnerable sense of happiness within and a steady vigor in your life even when things are not looking so good.

You have a sense of humor about life. A sign of humility and happiness is that you can laugh easily and enjoy an anecdote every now and then. When you laugh you improve your mood and lighten your heart from whatever burdens it. You have been doing it your whole life, and it is how you accept happiness in your life. Do what makes you happy, have fun with your hobbies and interests, and enjoy the people in your life who make you laugh until your stomach hurts when you socialize with them.

You can forgive yourself and apologize for the mistakes you make. You have made mistakes in every aspect of your life, and you are mature enough to admit and atone for it. It is so easy to accept happiness in your life when you are not busy keeping up a holier-than-thou image to yourself and others. You can say sorry and move on. Your humility is what keeps you emotionally healthy even if you have a lot to learn in relationships.

You can sleep at night. Your clean conscience is what allows you to approach every day with a new attitude and a fresh approach to life. Your acceptance of happiness in your life today is contingent on your release of all the drama that happened yesterday. Because you have faith in tomorrow, you are showing unconditional acceptance of the joy and happiness in your life and your will to learn to love again against all odds.

In the Name of God, the Most Trustworthy One on Whom We All Depend, the Source of Our Loving Divine Identity, the Loving One

Principles of Trust

Become trustworthy yourself. When your life becomes a reflection of good values and principles, it is easier to see them in others and attract them to yourself. Be honest, caring, understanding, and trustworthy yourself before you ask others to do the same. When you honestly try to uphold your word and honor as you enter relationships, your conscience is clear because you are putting forth your best effort to be a good person. Regardless of the outcome of your past relationships, learning to love again requires you to put your trust in God first and strive to be an upright person.

Don't worry about that which you cannot control. There are circumstances people encounter that are simply beyond their control. Becoming overly anxious and suspicious about what your loved ones are doing will make you miserable and destroy your peace of mind. Stay calm and try to think positive. Do something constructive with your time when you feel the anxiety of worrying come over you. There are times in your life when all you can do is pray and have faith that things will work out.

Do not spy or become overly suspicious of your loved ones. Respect your loved one's right to privacy and give him or her the benefit of the doubt. When you think your loved one might be guilty of something, it's easy to rationalize violating their privacy to find something that will justify your suspicion. Try talking to them instead of doing something conniving or sneaky. When you show security within yourself by not snooping on them, it is easier for your loved ones to trust and honor you.

Define your true identity. Your identity is not contingent on the perception others have of your relationship, career, and material acquisitions. Your identity is rooted in your inherent divine gifts and qualities from God Himself. You can learn to trust again when the outcome of a relationship will not compromise or destroy your self-worth and value to yourself.

Have patience with yourself and others. Accepting people for who they are is vital to building good, trusting relationships. Allowing yourself time to build a good friendship, free of intimacy, is key to building a solid committed relationship and marriage. There is no substitute for taking time to cultivate a friendship as the foundation of a committed relationship. When people genuinely like you and feel comfortable talking to you, they are willing to share more of themselves with you. Unfortunately, becoming romantically involved with someone does not eliminate the need to build a solid friendship with them first. It is often extremely difficult to trust someone when you feel they hardly know you and you hardly know them. It takes time to build good, trusting relationships, so have patience to make sure the foundation has been built on solid ground.

Learn to communicate better. In order to trust your partner it is important to learn to talk to each other to reach an understanding. Yelling accusations or getting highly emotional will not help you resolve any trust issues and will only make a situation worse. Calmly learn to express yourself and express your thoughts in a manner that makes you and your loved one feel comfortable. Open up and don't be afraid of being hurt again. Tear down your emotional walls. The walls that protect you from being hurt also prevent you from experiencing the joy of truly loving again. Once you know how and on whom to rely for your strength and support, there should be no fear in your heart of loving and trusting someone again.

Get counseling. Don't be afraid to talk to a trained professional for help in your current relationship and to help you heal from others in your past. Take your emotional well-being seriously and seek all the help you need to feel whole and happy again.

I want you to find love, happiness, and trust in your life. Learning to trust again is one of the most important steps in the process to learn to love again.

In the Name of God, the Originator of Thought, the Absolute All Within the Darkness that Worked Light into Existence Determined to Be the Light Himself

The Reawakening

Standing in the crossroads of time, we are faced with the daunting task of coming into a peaceful, happy realization of the dream of finding true love, which only the lucky seem to achieve. Within the spectrum of influences ranging from relationships to reality TV shows, our hopes of love can be dampened by unrealistic expectations put on us by ourselves and society. How do we turn off the confusion, the voices, the lies that tell us we had our chance to love, and that utopian prospect of happiness and joy has somehow slipped beyond our grasp? I'm here to show you, to prove to you that learning to love again is not only possible, it is real and achievable and just a thought away from burying within your heart a seed that will grow into real companionship and love right in your life.

Well, what's stopping the process of learning to love again? We are! First, we have to believe it is possible. In order to believe it we have to conceptualize it, visualize it, and internalize its spiritual nuances.

The exploration into the bountiful depths of our love experiences should give us the desire to find fulfillment in engaging in the process of learning to love again with a renewed enthusiasm. When we equated love with mere intimacy, we were really treating love as a contractual emotional commitment that required conditional expectations to be met constantly or the feeling itself, this emotional ecstasy, was dismissed as an illusion by us.

As long as the sensations of infatuation and romance are equated with love we are destined to be let down, disappointed, and heartbroken, because our perception of love is colored by immaturity and egotism. We have approached love with a selfish, instant-gratification mindset that leaves little or no room for trials, tribulations, disappointment, and most of all self-discovery to take place. The making of our character, the formation of our identities has been hinged on what our mood dictated to us as what love should feel like, what love should sound like, at any given moment.

Was it wrong to feel like that in our immaturity? NO. But after knowledge and wisdom comes to us, we must rise in maturity to meet it with the appropriate actions. We attain the fruits of wisdom, through prayer, study, and a patient determination to become a better reflection of the loving qualities of God in our everyday life. Unfortunately, we have been emotionally exploited to expect love to unfold as a Hollywood scene perfectly cast and directed, with no spiritual or character adjustment needed on our part. It is this perception of love — commercially fed to us from the mainstream media — that has us wanting all the benefits of a loving relationship without the willingness to put in the work to mold and shape ourselves through adversity, pain, and disappointment. To learn how to truly love again is to appreciate what it really means to develop patience, forbearance, strength, discipline, and an unshakeable spirit to succeed in love regardless of the circumstances.

In learning to love again we must remove the commercial influences in our lives, the chatter of friends and family, and even the religious community, which have us jumping through all kinds of financial and social hoops to be seen as someone "happy" in their eyes. Learning to love again requires first that you remember that love is not an emotion, it is the mother of emotions that God has placed in all of us as the source of inspiration, motivation and will to be nurturing, forgiving, charitable, benevolent, and merciful. It is not simply a feeling that can be altered by mood or circumstance. Love is manifested by the expressive will of the Creator Himself, and it is placed in us to be a conduit to reflect God's attributes of patience, mercy, and beneficence. Real love is eternal because it is the vibrant spirit within each and every one of us that forges us ahead to struggle through the darkness of loneliness, heartbreak and betrayal. When you embark on this journey to learn to love again, the identity of who you are—spiritually, morally, mentally, emotionally, and physically—is put on the road to self-improvement, self-development, and self-awareness.

When we are learning to accept our own and be ourselves, we start to resonate a vibrant spirit that attracts to us others with a similar disposition or spirit. Within this state the expression of real love can be manifested through us once we are tapping into the source of love, the author of our heavenly attributes, God Himself. An example of learning to love again is when we give a sincere smile intended not to seduce or manipulate but to inspire and encourage the one who receives it, regardless of what the person can do for us in return.

As a mother's love for her child is unconditional, learning to love again involves the realization that the love we have to give should be given with that same spirit: unconditional, unwavering, and unfaltering as God's love is for us. If a relationship called for separation or even severance, that does not mean that the qualities of God that you related to in that person are not worthy of your reciprocity and devotion. **All relationships require WORK to WORK OUT, and both parties must agree on what that WORK is and how it should be measured and quantified as indicators of the love between each other.**

So whether we find compatibility or not in our past should not deter us from tapping into the abundant source of love that illuminates our lives, the qualities of God in ourselves and others. We should celebrate to discover it within ourselves, because like a treasure with infinite value, we now know how to identify it in ourselves and can almost instantly recognize it others. So whether it is a sincere smile or a word of encouragement, learning to love again requires us to tap into the infinite within ourselves and share with others whose light might not be as bright or might be brighter than ours. We will never enjoy lasting peace until we shine real, substantive love into the darkness of our mind and hearts.

AFTERWARD
In the Name of God, the Powerful, the Restorer of Peace

Thank you for starting this journey to learn to love again and accept the challenge of overcoming the obstacles between healing, trusting, and, ultimately, opening your heart up to give and receive real love again. If you earnestly apply the principles in this book, you will witness a change within yourself that allows you to take whatever hardships you have experienced in relationships and learn to love again in a way that is fulfilling and unconditional.

Determined to become, with the help of God, a more loving person despite what has happened to me in my life, I developed into a witness and a student of the principles in this book. I am an ordinary person who has chosen to love in an extraordinary fashion that frees me from the fear and worry of the disappointment that relationships might bring. I am no different from you, and you too can make up your mind to learn and apply the steps and techniques in this book to become a witness-bearer to the power of love and God to heal you.

Many people have written to me to confide how instrumental these words have been in transforming their perception of love and relationships. All kinds of people, young and old, from different stations of life, have benefited from my work. Hopefully, if you complete this book you will no longer feel like a victim of love, and you'll feel better about all of your relationships, because you are learning to love again and growing spiritually and emotionally as a person as a result.

Acknowledgments

I would like first to thank God for giving me the inspiration and strength to learn to love again. Without Him none of this would be possible. I would like to thank all of my friends and family who listened, counseled, and gave me encouragement through my journey to learn to love again. This book was made possible by all the random smiles, warm hugs, and words of wisdom that were shared with me. I am eternally grateful to my editors for their patience with me to complete this project.

BIO

Are you stuck on a relationship treadmill? Numb to real emotion? Burned by misplacing your trust? Atlanta-based writer and entrepreneur Jameel Muhammad, after years of counseling his community of readers on affairs of the heart, now compiles his lessons of love, redemption, and spirituality for a wider audience.

A true practitioner of the maxim "healer, heal thyself," Jameel was inspired to help others learn to love again after he overcame the wounds of a painful divorce by applying the principles of this book. Along his journey of self-discovery, he discovered he could help others navigate the same relationship pitfalls he stumbled into.

A common man with a common-sense approach to life and healing, Jameel offers those who have gotten lost along the journey of relationships an easy-to-follow road map back to serenity and love.

Made in the USA
Columbia, SC
12 October 2023

24017128R00041